THE HISTORY OF
FORMULA ONE

BY ANTHONY K. HEWSON

SportsZone

An Imprint of Abdo Publishing
abdobooks.com

abdobooks.com

Published by Abdo Publishing, a division of ABDO, PO Box 398166, Minneapolis, Minnesota 55439. Copyright © 2024 by Abdo Consulting Group, Inc. International copyrights reserved in all countries. No part of this book may be reproduced in any form without written permission from the publisher. SportsZone™ is a trademark and logo of Abdo Publishing.

Printed in the United States of America, North Mankato, Minnesota.
052023
092023

Cover Photo: Bernard Cahier/Hulton Archive/Getty Images
Interior Photos: PA Images/Getty Images, 4; S&G/PA Images/Getty Images, 6; Bettman/Getty Images, 8–9; Keystone-France/Gamma-Keystone/Getty Images, 11; Hy Peskin/Archive Photos/Getty Images, 12; GP Library/Universal Images Group/Getty Images, 14–15; Bernard Cahier/Hulton Archive/Getty Images, 17; Paul-Henri Cahier/Hulton Archive/Getty Images, 19, 22; John Marsh/EMPICS/ PA Images/Getty Images, 20; Clive Mason/Getty Images Sport/Getty Images, 25; Mark Thompson/Getty Images Sport/Getty Images, 26; Peter J. Fox/Getty Images Sport/Getty Images, 27; Alex Pantling/Formula 1/Getty Images, 29

Editor: Charlie Beattie
Series Designer: Michael J. Williams

Library of Congress Control Number: 2022949079

Publisher's Cataloging-in-Publication Data

Names: Hewson, Anthony K., author.
Title: The history of formula one / by Anthony K. Hewson
Description: Minneapolis, Minnesota: Abdo Publishing Company, 2024 | Series: Focus on formula one | Includes online resources and index.
Identifiers: ISBN 9781098290771 (lib. bdg.) | ISBN 9781098276959 (ebook)
Subjects: LCSH: Formula One automobiles--Juvenile literature. | Automobiles, Racing--History--Juvenile literature. | Sports car racing--Juvenile literature.
Classification: DDC 796.72--dc23

TABLE OF CONTENTS

King George VI, *left*, shakes hands with English driver Reg Parnell before the start of the 1950 British Grand Prix.

CHAPTER ONE

WHERE IT ALL BEGAN

A crowd of 120,000 people came out to England's Silverstone Circuit on May 13, 1950. They were there to witness the start of something big. Even King George VI of the United Kingdom was on hand for the first race in the new Formula One World Championship, organized by the International Automobile Federation (FIA). But none of them knew the sport would still be going strong more than 70 years later.

Formula One racing looked quite different back then. Drivers wore cloth caps and goggles for safety. The winning car reached just 350 horsepower. That's roughly one-third as powerful as Formula One cars today.

Driving race cars was not a full-time career like it is today. The field in Silverstone included a jazz musician and a prince of Thailand. Race winner Dr. Giuseppe "Nino" Farina was a doctor of political science.

Crews inspect their cars before the 1950 British Grand Prix.

Farina drove one of four Alfa Romeo cars entered in the race. Alfa had a proud racing history, and its four drivers were favorites to win. The quality of the rest of the field varied widely. The distance between first and last place in qualifying was 18 seconds. That gap today is usually closer to three seconds. The top racing speed in 1950 was 180 miles per hour (290 km/h). Today's cars reach 220 miles per hour (354 km/h).

Farina outdueled teammate and fellow Italian Luigi Fagioli for the win. The final victory margin was 2.6 seconds. Englishman Reg Parnell was a distant third, 52 seconds back. The crowd that day

Giuseppe Farina crosses the finish line in first place as an official waves the checkered flag at the 1950 British Grand Prix.

went home as witnesses to the first-ever thrilling day of Formula One racing.

A WINNING FORMULA

The 1950 season was the official beginning of the sport beloved around the world today as Formula One. But motor racing had begun decades earlier. There were many steps on the way to making Formula One what it is today.

The term "grand prix" means "grand prize" in French. It was first used as the name of a car race in 1901. The FIA was formed in 1904. The modern practice of determining qualifying position for a race based on lap time began in 1933.

Auto racing was common across Europe, but it took many different forms. Attempts to keep a racing series going were complicated by the outbreak of World War I (1914–18) and

World War II (1939–45). After World War II ended, interest in a racing series picked up again.

In 1946 participants created a set of rules that everyone had to agree on. These rules and regulations are the "formula" in Formula One. The rules covered everything from the size of the engine to what drivers had to wear. Those original rules have changed in countless ways over the years to keep Formula One exciting and on the cutting edge of technology. However, the spirit of the original racers lives on in the sport today.

Farina, *center*, finished the 1950 British Grand Prix in 2 hours, 13 minutes, and 23 seconds.

Juan Manuel Fangio won 24 Grand Prix races between 1950 and 1958, a record that stood for 10 years.

CHAPTER TWO

TECH TRIUMPHS AND TRAGEDIES

No one team was dominant during the early days of Formula One. But there were dominant drivers. Juan Manuel Fangio of Argentina raced in just seven full Formula One seasons between 1950 and 1958. But he won the drivers' championship in five of them. And he did so with four different teams, as manufacturers were just beginning to establish themselves.

The constructors' championship was awarded for the first time in 1958. This meant that manufacturing teams as well as their drivers could compete to be the best in the world. The first race

Jackie Stewart, *left,* tries to chase down Graham Hill, *right,* at the 1965 Monaco Grand Prix.

of the 1958 season was in Fangio's home country of Argentina. But it was English driver Stirling Moss who stole the show. Up until 1958, no driver had won a race in a rear-engine car. Moss became the first. The win helped make rear-engine cars standard in Formula One.

Moss was one of many successful drivers from the United Kingdom in the 1950s, 1960s,

and 1970s. The country has a proud racing history.
From 1962 to 1973, British Formula One teams
won 12 world championships. Many of those
winning cars were piloted by drivers such
as Scotsman Jackie Stewart and Englishman
Graham Hill.

Technology was a big part of that success. Colin
Chapman was the founder of Team Lotus. He was

also an engineer and designer. Lotus introduced the revolutionary monocoque chassis in 1962. The design made the chassis one single piece rather than multiple components. It helped both the strength and handling of the car. Formula One cars are still made with these same principles.

Lotus was also the first team to accept a sponsor on one of its cars in 1968. Racing is an expensive sport. The sponsorship helped cover some of those costs. Today, sponsorship is a massive part of a Formula One team's revenue.

AIR POWER

Racing teams had known the effects of air on cars for some time. But until the 1970s, teams were mostly worried about air slowing cars down. Chapman and Lotus designed a car that harnessed the air to push a car onto the track.

The pressure helped the car take turns at higher speeds and handle better. This concept is called downforce.

The Lotus 72 car won two drivers' world championships and three constructors' championships between 1970 and 1973. Downforce soon became a priority for Formula One teams. Teams tried to design cars with as much downforce as possible. But these setups

Emerson Fittipaldi takes a corner in the revolutionary Lotus 72 car at the 1972 Spanish Grand Prix.

could be dangerous. A slight miscalculation could make the car hard to control.

Throughout the 1970s and 1980s, Formula One became increasingly popular. Drivers such as Emerson Fittipaldi, James Hunt, and Niki Lauda dominated the 1970s. But the sport was becoming controversially dangerous. Risk of injury and death had always been a part of Formula One. Between 1952 and 1979, 41 drivers lost their lives. The sport struggled to keep up with safety. Full-face helmets weren't mandatory

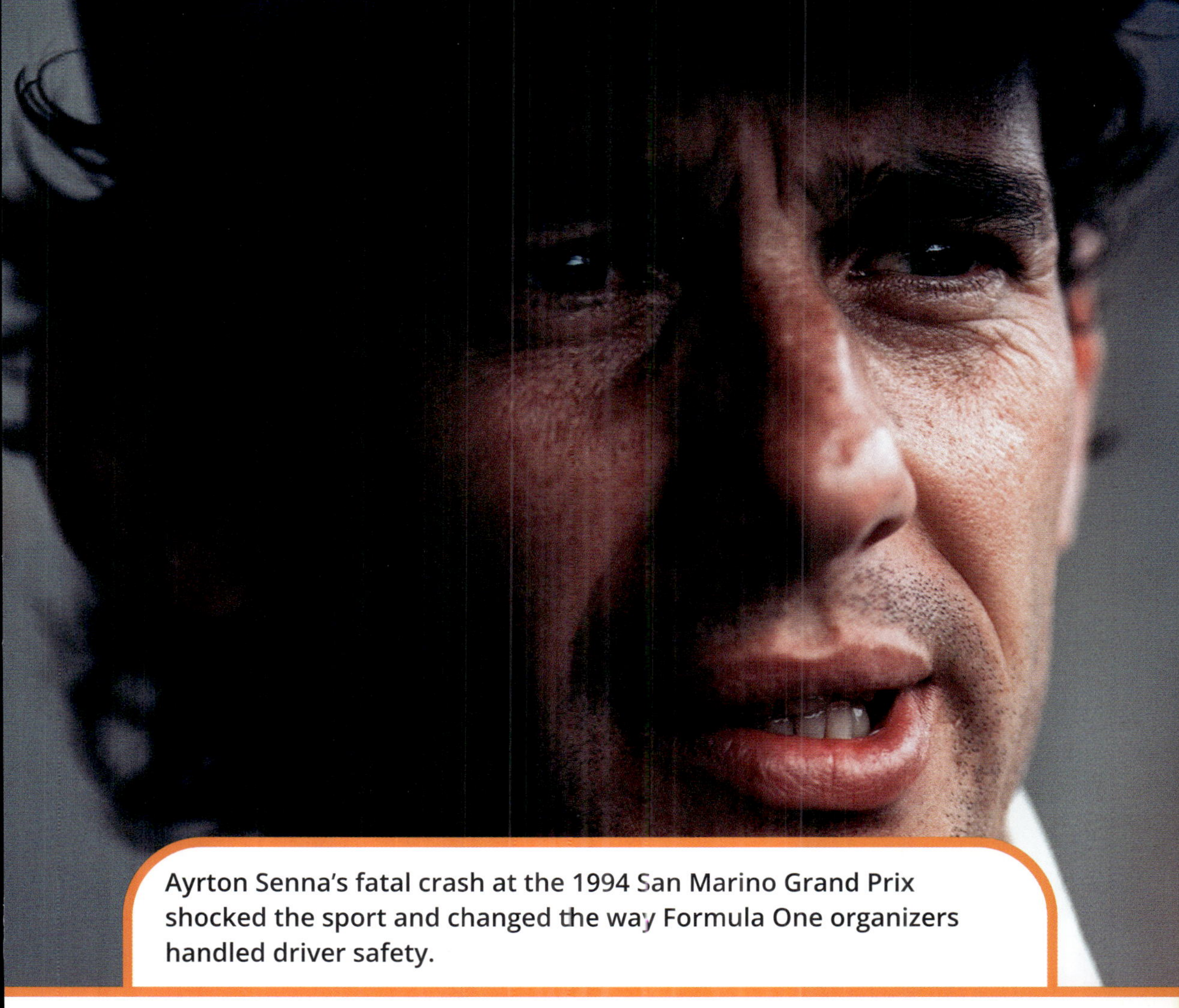

Ayrton Senna's fatal crash at the 1994 San Marino Grand Prix shocked the sport and changed the way Formula One organizers handled driver safety.

until the early 1970s. Drivers didn't have to wear flame-resistant suits until 1975.

By the 1980s, a new group of stars had taken over. Alain Prost, his teammate and rival Ayrton Senna, and Englishman Nigel Mansell dominated

Mika Häkkinen won the Formula One drivers' championship in 1998 and 1999.

until the mid-1990s. Soon, however, track deaths would once again change Formula One. Austrian driver Roland Ratzenberger died after a crash in qualifying at the 1994 San Marino Grand Prix. The extremely popular Senna died from injuries suffered in a crash at the race the next day.

The terrible weekend led to several rule changes. Downforce was reduced so cars could not take corners at such dangerous speeds. Tracks were redesigned to have more space. And drivers soon had to wear devices that restrained their heads and necks in the event of a crash.

The 1994 season ended with German Michael Schumacher winning his first drivers' championship. For the rest of the 1990s, he battled Englishman Damon Hill and Finland's Mika Häkkinen for racing dominance as Formula One soared again.

Bernie Ecclestone was the chief executive of Formula One for 40 years before stepping down in 2017.

CHAPTER THREE

A NEW CENTURY

n 1958 English driver Bernie Ecclestone tried to enter two Formula One races. He didn't qualify for either one. That was the end of Ecclestone's driving career. He stayed in the sport, however, eventually buying the Brabham team in 1971. Throughout the decade Ecclestone grew more powerful in the sport. He eventually rose to run Formula One itself. Ecclestone's savvy business decisions helped make the series a multibillion-dollar business by the year 2000.

Ecclestone was still running Formula One behind the scenes into the 2000s. But on the track, the races belonged to German superstar Michael Schumacher. By 2004 Schumacher had won seven drivers' championships. He won his record 52nd career Grand Prix in 2001. When he retired for good in 2012, Schumacher had 91 wins.

Almost all those victories came in a Ferrari. The Italian company was one of several large car manufacturers now dominating the sport. Smaller independent teams such as Lotus were becoming rare as they struggled to compete financially.

THE GOLDEN ERA

Schumacher's wins also came in a powerful V-10 engine, which Formula One used between 1996 and 2005. Over the next decade, the engines shrank to become V-8s and then V-6s. However, they also became more efficient. Other technical innovations helped streamline the cars to increase

Michael Schumacher won a then-record 13 races during the 2004 season.

their speed. Passing at races became more common. The races themselves became wide open and thrilling.

Advertisers flocked to Formula One. Energy drink manufacturer Red Bull went so far as to create its own team. Many dismissed the move as a marketing gimmick at first. But Red Bull soon became a powerhouse. It competed with established teams such as McLaren and Ferrari.

Mercedes also returned to Formula One in 2010 after 55 years away.

Those teams were stocked with a new cast of excellent young drivers. Formula One crowned its youngest champion ever three times over six years in the 2000s. Spanish driver Fernando Alonso was just 24 when he won in 2005. Three years later, 23-year-old Englishman Lewis Hamilton won his first title. German Sebastian Vettel was also 23 when he won in 2010, 167 days younger than Hamilton had been.

Sebastian Vettel won nine straight races during the 2013 season.

Lewis Hamilton won at least nine Grand Prix races every year from 2014 through 2020.

Hamilton and Vettel ruled the sport in the 2010s. Racing with Red Bull, Vettel won four straight drivers' championships. Hamilton won six titles in seven years for Mercedes between 2014 and 2020. His only second place was to teammate Nico Rosburg. Along the way, Hamilton smashed Schumacher's record for Grand Prix victories.

Another young star emerged in the late 2010s to challenge Hamilton's dominance. Max Verstappen of the Netherlands was just 17 when he first raced in Formula One in 2015. Within four years, he was a title challenger.

In 2021 both Verstappen and Hamilton had a chance to win the championship heading into the final race. Verstappen passed Hamilton on the final lap of the Abu Dhabi Grand Prix to claim victory in one of the sport's most dramatic seasons ever. The tight finish also fueled the growing rivalry between the two drivers.

Max Verstappen moved into sixth place in all-time Formula One wins in 2022, at the age of only 25.

As teams, Red Bull and Mercedes were pulling away from the field. Other rule changes in 2022 made cars more aerodynamic and faster in traffic. The idea was to make racing more competitive again. However, Verstappen dominated the 2022 season. His 15 wins set a new season record.

As Formula One continued its efforts to make the sport more competitive, fans were still tuning in. The sport made over $2.6 billion in 2022. And with drivers and innovators continuing to take entertaining chances, the future looked bright.

GLOSSARY

aerodynamic
Relating to the forces of air acting on a car.

chassis
The main part of a car, where the engine and suspension are attached.

drivers' championship
A title that is awarded each year to the Formula One driver who earns the most points throughout the racing season.

horsepower
A measure of power of an engine, with one horsepower equaling 746 watts.

independent
Not belonging to a larger organization.

innovator
Someone who has new ideas about how something can be done.

qualifying
A process to determine the starting order for a race.

sponsor
An advertiser that pays money to have its name or logo on a product.

MORE INFORMATION

BOOKS

Hewson, Anthony K. *Formula One Grand Prix Races*. Minneapolis, MN: Abdo Publishing, 2024.

Hustad, Douglas. *Innovations in Auto Racing*. Minneapolis, MN: Abdo Publishing, 2022.

Rule, Heather. *GOATs of Auto Racing*. Minneapolis, MN: Abdo Publishing, 2022.

ONLINE RESOURCES

To learn more about Formula One history, please visit **abdobooklinks.com** or scan this QR code. These links are routinely monitored and updated to provide the most current information available.

INDEX

ABOUT THE AUTHOR

Anthony K. Hewson is a freelance writer originally from San Diego. He and his wife now live in the San Francisco Bay Area with their two dogs.